POSEIDON

RUSSIA'S NEW DOOMSDAY MACHINE

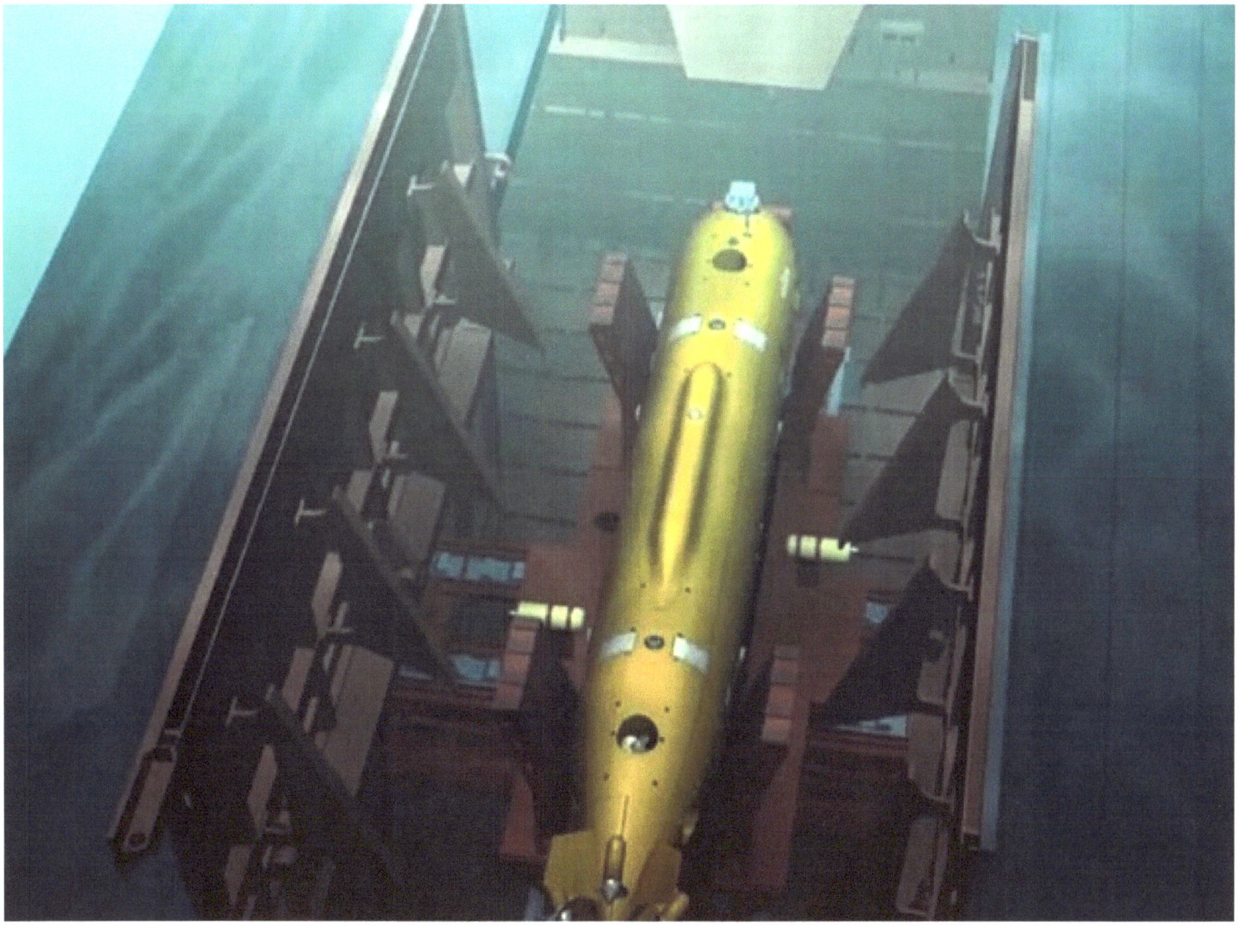

Dr. Peter Vincent Pry

EMP Task Force on National and Homeland Security

2018

OTHER BOOKS AND REPORTS BY THE
EMP TASK FORCE ON NATIONAL AND HOMELAND SECURITY
ARE AVAILABLE FROM
AMAZON.COM

THE LONG SUNDAY

BLACKOUT WARS

APOCALYPSE UNKNOWN

ELECTRIC ARMAGEDDON

EXECUTIVE SUMMARY

- Russia's POSEIDON is a nuclear super-weapon now undergoing testing, comprising an unmanned automated drone submarine that can travel intercontinental distances and defeat U.S. anti-submarine capabilities by speed, stealth, and elusiveness, to deliver a 100-megaton warhead, by far the most powerful nuclear weapon in existence.

- POSEIDON's advertised mission is to destroy U.S. coastal regions, ports, and aircraft carriers by detonating underwater to raise nuclear tsunamis and spread radioactive fallout.

- In 1961, Moscow tested a nuclear super-weapon called TSAR designed to yield 100-150 megatons and make enormous amounts of radioactive fallout, like POSEIDON.

- POSEIDON's advertised mission to destroy U.S. coasts, ports, and aircraft carriers may be disinformation, as the machine is unsuited for these purposes, which can be better accomplished by a single Russian ballistic missile submarine and other existing forces.

- POSEIDON makes more military sense as a hunter-killer to destroy U.S. ballistic missile submarines (SSBNs) on patrol at sea, normally numbering 7 today and 6 in the future (down from dozens during the Cold War), as this most survivable leg of the Triad could be vulnerable to the underwater shockwave from a 100-megaton explosion.

- POSEIDON could be an elaborate disinformation campaign to conceal the real purpose of revival of a 100-megaton TSAR-like warhead, which makes most military sense for high-altitude electromagnetic pulse (EMP) attack to paralyze U.S. forces—including SSBNs on patrol—and win a war at a single blow, and as a doomsday weapon that could kill 90 percent of the U.S. population, eliminating America as an actor on the world stage.

- POSEIDON is the latest in a series of Russian doomsday weapons, including TSAR, DEAD HAND, and VRYAN, whose revelation in each case historically is associated with perceptions by Moscow of an extreme international crisis verging on nuclear war.

- If POSEIDON combines nuclear super-weapons with Artificial Intelligence, it is an unprecedented new threat that eclipses the invention of the atomic bomb.

- **The U.S. should EMP harden critical infrastructures, deploy space-based missile defenses, modernize strategic forces, develop new generation nuclear weapons, sink POSEIDON if deployed to autonomously patrol the oceans as an artificially intelligent doomsday machine—and through these acts of strength seek a New Détente and real strategic partnership with Russia, as should have resulted from the end of the old Cold War.**

5

POSEIDON:

Russia's New Doomsday Machine

Doomsday now has a name. The Russian Defense Ministry has christened their newest nuclear apocalypse machine "POSEIDON"—after the Greek God of oceans, earthquakes, and tsunamis.

POSEIDON will be deployed between 2018 and 2027, according to TASS. The doomsday robot-sub development program, until now known by the code-name "KANYON", was secret until disclosed in 2016.[1]

In 2016, Russian state television "accidentally" revealed plans for an unmanned robot submarine, like a huge intelligent torpedo, reportedly armed with a massive 100-megaton warhead—the largest nuclear weapon ever deployed by any nation. The submarine doomsday bomb would explode underwater to radioactively contaminate and inundate with tsunamis U.S. coastal cities and seaboard, where are concentrated much of America's military-industrial strength and population.[2]

A diagram of the robot-bomb was shown on Russian TV, supposedly inadvertently, over the shoulder of a Defense Ministry officer.[3]

U.S. intelligence confirms the existence of POSEIDON in the 2018 Nuclear Posture Review (NPR). According to the NPR, Russia is testing a prototype of the unmanned robot submarine designed to deliver its doomsday bomb.[4]

A former senior Defense Department official, Dr. Mark Schneider, who is one of Washington's most astute and best informed analysts, told ace reporter Bill Gertz of the Washington Free Beacon that, according to Russian reports, the power of the robot-bomb will be 100 megatons— equivalent to 100 million tons of TNT.[5]

The Russian press agency TASS, notorious for disinformation, recently reports the yield of POSEIDON is "up to 2 megatons" contradicting earlier Russian reports that the yield is 100 megatons.[6] 2 megatons is not an unusually high yield for a Russian nuclear weapon, is in the average range. Nor is a 2-megaton yield for POSEIDON consistent with Russian dictator Vladimir Putin's description (in his March 1, 2018 televised briefing to the world on Russia's

---

[1] "Russian Navy To Get Poseidon Nuclear Underwater Drones By 2027" Russian Ministry of Defense (May 12, 2018) http://tass.com/defense/1003964. See also "Putin: New Weapons Will Maintain Russia's Might For Decades" Associated Press (May 15, 2018) http://tass.com/defense/1004464. Vladimir Isachenko, "Putin: New Nuclear Weapons To Enter Duty In Next Few Years" Associated Press for Chicago Tribune (May 22, 2018).

[2] Bill Gertz, "Russia Tests Nuclear-Capable Drone Sub" The Gertz File (December 8, 2016).

[3] Ibid.

[4] Bill Gertz, "Pentagon Confirms Russia Building Underwater Nuclear Drone" Washington Free Beacon (January 17, 2018). Bill Gertz, "Putin Unveils Nuclear-Powered Cruise Missiles, Drone Submarines For Attacking U.S." Washington Free Beacon (March 2, 2018).

[5] Gertz, op. cit. (December 8, 2016).

[6] "Underwater Drone To Be Equipped With Nuclear Warhead" TASS (May 21, 2018).

POSEIDON

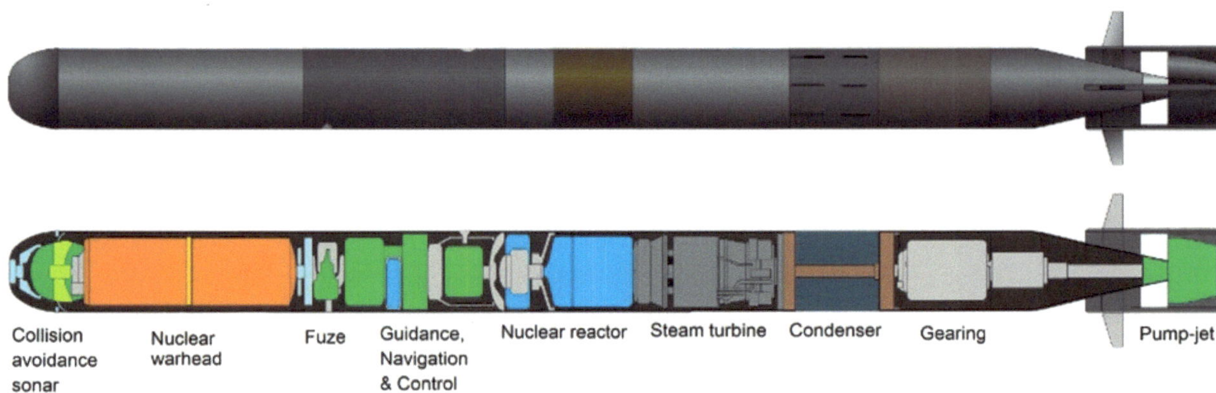

new nuclear super-weapons) that the robot-bomb carries a "massive nuclear ordinance." Nor could a 2-megaton warhead likely raise tsunamis 300 feet high, as advertised. Photographs of the POSEIDON prototype now being tested show a vessel that appears capable of accommodating a very big warhead of 100 megatons.[7]

The contractor heading project POSEIDON, Alexei Rakhmanov, told Interfax on May 23, 2018, "Russia will not publish the characteristics of the unmanned nuclear submarine Poseidon." And "I cannot say more than the president said."[8]

"On March 1, the Russian president spoke about the creation in Russia of unmanned underwater machines capable of moving at a very low depth and at intercontinental range at a speed far exceeding the speed of submarines, the most modern torpedoes and all types of surface ships, even the most high-speed ones," Interfax accurately reports, paraphrasing Vladimir Putin.[9]

According to POSEIDON contractor Rakhmanov, Russia's doomsday robot-bomb is "not a fantasy, not a prototype and it's not a cartoon. These machines really exist."[10]

What to make of this Strangelovian threat from Moscow?

Even if Russia's doomsday robot-sub is disinformation to frighten the West with a shock and awe boogeyman, it is no laughing matter. This new threat, even if fictional, manifests a paranoid hostility and recklessness worse than anything from the Cold War. East and West are supposed to have moved beyond the Cold War and learned not to repeat its worst mistakes.

Yet Moscow is telling us the Cold War is back in deep freeze. They are thinking about 1950s-type all-out thermonuclear mass destruction of entire peoples and nations. After blasting us into oblivion, they would sow our soil with radioactive salt so there could be no recovery.

Unfortunately, Russia's 100-megaton doomsday bomb is real.

The Doomsday Bomb: TSAR

Moscow built a 100-megaton bomb called the TSAR BOMBA ("King of Bombs" officially the RDS-220), tested the day before Halloween, on October 30, 1961. TSAR was deliberately tested to only half strength, 50-60 megatons, by removing the third stage. No bomber could survive if TSAR were tested to full strength. And at 100 megatons the TSAR would have covered vast swaths of Russia with radioactive fallout, though tested in far Novaya Zemlya beyond the Arctic Circle.[11]

TSAR was a three-stage thermonuclear weapon. The first stage used fission to compress a thermonuclear second stage, just like in a normal H-bomb, except the first and second stages

---

[7] "Putin Presented Poseidon A Nuclear-Armed Underwater Drone…" www.youtube.com/watch?v=dOB_IdTeen4
[8] "Characteristics Of Unmanned Nuclear Submarine Poseidon To Remain Secret" Interfax (May 23, 2018). See also "Undersea Warfare News" http://www.subforce.navy.mil/
[9] Ibid.
[10] Ibid.
[11] "Big Ivan, The Tsar Bomba ('King of Bombs'): The World's Largest Nuclear Weapon" nuclearweaponarchive.org (September 3, 2007). "Tsar Bomba" Wikipedia.

were more powerful, yielding 50-60 megatons, already twice as powerful as the biggest U.S. H-bomb ever built.[12]

TSAR's thermonuclear second stage was designed to compress another thermonuclear third stage and to fission a uranium tamper. All three stages would release an estimated 100-150 megatons. The third stage would also, by fissioning uranium, produce enormous amounts of radioactive fallout.[13]

As noted above, when testing TSAR the third stage was removed to give the bomber crew some chance of survival, reducing the tested yield to 50-60 megatons, and eliminating most of the radioactive fallout, which would have posed a grave threat to Russia.[14]

TSAR is the most powerful nuclear weapon ever built, even at half strength yielding the biggest explosion ever produced by mankind—releasing more than 10 times the energy of all the ordnance exploded in World War II. 100 megatons is energetically equivalent to 10,000 Hiroshima A-bombs or 1,000 U.S. W80 H-bombs (yield 100 kilotons). The most powerful bomb ever deployed by the U.S. is the B41 (yield 25 megatons) scrapped in 1976.[15]

When testing the TSAR—even though tested only to half strength—the Soviets estimated their bomber crew only had a 50 percent chance of surviving its blast and thermal effects. Its enormous fireball was visible at a distance of 1,000 kilometers (620 miles). TSAR's shockwave was observed rippling the atmosphere at a distance of 700 kilometers (430 miles).[16]

Moscow tested TSAR over the wastelands of Novaya Zemlya, a remote island surrounded by the Arctic Ocean, to isolate its effects from the Russian mainland and humanity. All buildings within the test range, both wooden and brick, were destroyed, including the village of Severny located 55 kilometers (34 miles) from ground zero. The thermal pulse would have caused third degree burns at a distance of 100 kilometers (62 miles) and was felt by an observer 270 kilometers (170 miles) from ground zero. Windows and doors were broken at a distance from ground zero of 900 kilometers (560 miles), including in Finland and Sweden.[17]

Even though TSAR was not a ground contact burst, but airburst at an altitude of 4 kilometers (13,000 feet), it caused an earthquake-like seismic shockwave, registering at 5.5, that circled the planet three times.[18]

If TSAR was tested to its full 100-megaton yield, instead of half-strength, its energy would be equivalent to 10 percent of all nuclear weapons ever tested. Radioactive fallout from TSAR's

---

[12] Ibid. "Tsar Bomba" Atomic Heritage Foundation (July 29, 2016).

[13] Ibid. "50th Anniversary of Tsar Bomb" Russia Today International (October 30, 2011).

[14] Ibid.

[15] Ibid. "Moscow's Biggest Bomb: The 50-Megaton Test Of October 1961" *Cold War International History Project Bulletin* (October 7, 2011).

[16] Ibid. Stephen Dowling, "The Monster Atomic Bomb That Was Too Big To Use" BBC (August 16, 2017).

[17] Ibid. Vitaliy Khalturin, Tatyana Rautian, Paul Richards, William Leith, "A Review Of Nuclear Testing By The Soviet Union At Novaya Zemlya, 1955-1990" Science and Global Security (2005). Central Intelligence Agency, "Soviet Atomic Energy Program" National Intelligence Estimate (May 16, 1962).

[18] Ibid. "Tsar Bomba's Blast Wave Orbited Earth Three Times In 1961" Pravda (September 17, 2009).

third stage, that was not tested, would have been 25 percent of all radioactive fallout from all nuclear weapons ever tested.[19]

TSAR made such an impression on Andrei Sakharov, who was on the bomb's design team, that thereafter he became an outspoken opponent of nuclear weapons and the USSR's most famous political dissident.[20]

Psychopathy Of Gigantism

Moscow never deployed TSAR as an operational weapon because at 60,000 pounds (30 tons) it was too heavy for delivery by bombers trying to penetrate U.S. air defenses or for any missile at the time. TSAR was also militarily impractical for blasting cities and spreading fallout because this could be done more cost-effectively with numerous smaller nuclear weapons.[21]

If the same nuclear materials used to build the TSAR were used instead to build many smaller H-bombs, the net destructive capability would be greater. Moreover, smaller nuclear weapons could be delivered by bombers and missiles.

Indeed, according to U.S. calculations of "equivalent yield" the TSAR is a bad investment. The "equivalent yield" of a warhead having a yield (Y) less than one megaton is Y to the two-thirds power, whereas a warhead having a yield over one megaton is Y to the one-half power. According to this math, 10 one megaton warheads supposedly could do as much blast damage as the 100-megaton TSAR.[22]

Truth in advertising, "equivalent yield" was used by U.S. arms controllers during the Cold War to dismiss Russia's big advantage in high-yield weapons, and to argue for U.S. weapons of low yield. Despite the best efforts of U.S. arms controllers to "educate" Moscow, Russia always preferred having weapons of higher yield than the United States.[23]

So why did Moscow build and test the TSAR?

Part of the explanation may be that totalitarian and authoritarian regimes, especially those led by a megalomaniac, have a tendency toward what might be called the "psychopathy of gigantism" in public works and military weapons—even if they are impractical. The "great leader" of enormous ego and messianic aspiration, in every civilization throughout history, wants to build outsize monuments to himself. Objects that will overawe subjects, terrorize and cow enemies, and immortalize the "great leader" in the memory of Man.

The Pyramids of Egypt and monuments of Ramses, the Great Wall of China, and the Palace of Versailles are a few examples of such works.

---

[19] Ibid.

[20] Ibid. Andrei Sakharov, *Memoirs* (New York: Alfred Knopf, 1990).

[21] Dowling, op. cit.; "Tsar Bomba" Atomic Heritage Foundation op. cit; "Tsar Bomba" Wikipedia op. cit.

[22] Dr. Peter Vincent Pry, *The Strategic Nuclear Balance: And Why It Matters*, see chapter on "Equivalent Yield" (New York and London: Taylor & Francis, 1990).

[23] Ibid.

Tyrants and dictators, the man at the top of the pyramid of power, tend to like giant weapons too, even if they are militarily impractical. Perhaps the psychology of one-man rule biases the dictator to identify with his giant weapon, a singularity dominating the battlefield, as the dictator dominates his nation. He wants his monster to live and win, even if his scientists and generals warn him the giant is a waste of resources.[24]

So in 1586 Russia built the Tsar Cannon, weighing 40 tons with a bore one-yard wide, inscribed for "The grace of God, Tsar and Great Duke Fyodor Ivanovich Autocrat of all Great Russia." The Tsar Cannon, too heavy to move, never saw battle.[25]

Mehmed the Conqueror, Sultan of the Ottoman Empire, during his medieval siege of Constantinople in 1453, had a giant bombard requiring 60 oxen to move, 400 men three hours to load, that could throw a 600 pound stone one mile. Reports conflict over whether the great Dardanelles Gun blew itself up.[26]

Hitler commissioned the Great Gustav railway gun, weighing 1,350 tons and able to hurl a shell weighing seven tons 29 miles, which did good service at the siege of Sevastopol, but otherwise was a huge drain on scarce German resources.[27] The Nazi dictator also had plans for the biggest tank ever conceived, the Land Monitor, weighing 1,000 tons, too large and heavy for roads and bridges, that would wade rivers and roll across fields and forests like a mobile steel fortress—a perfect target for Allied airpower.[28]

Everyone knows the tragic fates of Hitler's giant battleship the *Bismarck* and the pride of the Japanese Navy, the *Yamato*, the largest battleship ever built, whose enormous 18-inch guns could out-range U.S. 16-inch guns by miles.[29] As a child, I could not understand, it seemed impossible and somehow unjust, that giant battleships could be such easy prey to tiny aircraft and torpedoes. Military dictatorships are likeminded, it seems, and never grow up.

Now Russian dictator Vladimir Putin apparently has taken out of mothballs the design of Russia's gigantic H-bomb.

Can We Thank Arms Control For The Doomsday Bomb?

Dictator Putin and his General Staff may see some practical reasons for bringing back the TSAR. Nuclear weapons now play a more important role in Russia's military doctrine for warfighting,

---

[24] Mikhail Popov, "Super-Weapons In The History Of Mankind" Mir Fantastiki (Moscow: August 2005, in Russian).

[25] Ibid. Mina Klein, *The Kremlin: Citadel of History* (New York: MacMillan, 1990). "Tsar Cannon" Wikipedia.

[26] Paul Hammer, *Warfare In Early Modern Europe 1450-1660* (Ashgate Publishing, 2007). Charles Ffoulkes, "The Dardanelles Gun At The Tower" Antiquarian Journal, Vol 10 (1930). "Dardanelles Gun" Wikipedia.

[27] Steven Zaloga and Peter Dennis, *Railway Guns of World War II* (Oxford, UK: Osprey Publishing, 2016). "Schewerer Gustav" Wikipedia (January 2016).

[28] David Porter, *Hitler's Secret Weapons 1933-1945* (London, UK: Amber Books, 2010). Peter Chamberlain and Hilary Doyle *Encyclopedia of German Tanks of World War Two* (Leicestershire, UK: Silverdale Books, 2004). "Landkreuzer P. 1000 Ratte" Wikipedia (August 2017).

[29] Robert Jackson, *The World's Great Battleships* (Brown Books, 2000). Hansgeorge Jentschura, Dieter Jung, Peter Mickel, *Warships of the Imperial Japanese Navy 1869-1945* (Annapolis, MD: U.S. Naval Institute, 1977). "German battleship Bismarck" and "Japanese Battleship Yamato" Wikipedia.

deterrence, and diplomacy than they did during the Cold War.[30] Russia is pouring resources into its nuclear forces, increasing their budget by 50 percent.[31]

But Russia faces limits on how many nuclear weapons it can deploy under the New Strategic Arms Reduction Treaty (New START) that limits Russia and the U.S. to 1,550 nuclear warheads on missiles and bombers.[32]

New START may be driving Russia to emphasize quality over quantity by, in addition to modernizing its missiles and bombers, building one or a few super-weapons like the TSAR. This would enable Moscow to stay within the New START limits while surging ahead of the U.S. technologically with a new class of super-bomb to overawe the U.S. and its allies.

Moreover, Russia has lots of weapons-grade nuclear fuels in storage, laying around unused, from thousands of warheads dismantled under START, and nuclear weapons factories that need work. TSAR can harness these materials and talent to useful purpose.[33]

Furthermore, the robot submarine proposed as the means to deliver TSAR may not, Moscow could argue, be covered by New START. POSEIDON is not a missile or a bomber. Arguably, it is a big nuclear mine, and may be categorized as a tactical nuclear weapon, despite its enormous yield, and therefore not limited by New START.[34]

However, Dr. Schneider correctly observes that Russia is already building warheads beyond the New START limits and predicts Moscow plans to breakout of New START.[35] Moscow has a long history of violating arms control treaties.

Therefore, New START calculations may have nothing to do with Russia's resurrection of the TSAR.

As an aside, the Trump Administration should declassify President Reagan's still classified General Advisory Committee full report *A Quarter Century of Soviet Compliance Practices Under Arms Control Commitments: 1958-1983* to finally explode the myth that arms control agreements with Russia serve America's national security interests. Moscow always cheats.[36]

---

[30]U.S. Department of Defense, *Nuclear Posture Review 2018* (Washington, DC: March 6, 2018). Katarzyna Zysk, "Escalation and Nuclear Weapons in Russia's Military Strategy" RUSI Journal (May 25, 2018). Dr. Mark Schneider, *The Nuclear Forces and Doctrine of the Russian Federation* (Washington, DC: United States Nuclear Strategy Forum, National Institute Press, 2006).

[31] "Russia To Up Nuclear Weapons Spending 50% By 2016" Sputnik: Military and Intelligence (October 8, 2013). Bill Gertz, "Russia Doubling Nuclear Warheads" Washington Free Beacon (April 1, 2016).

[32] U.S. Department of State, *New START* https://www.state.gov/t/avc/newstart/index.htm

[33] Russia has so much surplus weapons-grade nuclear uranium, the U.S. initiated a program to buy the surplus, now discontinued. See Oleg Bukharin and Helen Hunt, "The U.S.-Russia HEU Agreement" Science and Global Security, Vol. 4 (1994). "Megatons to Megawatts Program" Wikipedia (February 2009).

[34] Steven Pifer, "Arms Control Options for Non-Strategic Nuclear Weapons" Brookings (April 18, 2012). Tom Nichols, Douglas Stuart, Jeffrey McCausland, *Tactical Nuclear Weapons and NATO* (U.S. Army War College Strategic Studies Institute, 2017).

[35] Dr. Mark Schneider, *The Russian Nuclear Weapons Buildup and the Future of the New START Treaty* (National Institute for Public Policy, October 27, 2016).

[36] The unclassified executive summary of *A Quarter Century of Soviet Compliance Practices Under Arms Control*

Nuclear Tsunamis?

POSEIDON's chief purpose is to raise a tsunami, hundreds of feet high, that could flood and devastate U.S. coastal areas, according to Russian sources. Popularly, at least in most western press reporting, the notion of a nuclear tsunami is the most frightening aspect of POSEIDON.

Some scientists doubt a nuclear tsunami is possible.

Gregg Spriggs of Lawrence Livermore National Laboratory claims a nuclear tsunami is impossible (in an article titled "A Physicist Says Blowing Up Nuclear Weapons In The Ocean To Trigger Tsunamis Would Be Completely Stupid"). According to Spriggs, even a 100-megaton underwater explosion could not make a tsunami because natural tsunamis, like Japan's 2011 tsunami that killed over 15,000 people, are created by earthquakes that are energetically equivalent to thousands of megatons.[37]

Spriggs also notes that the U.S. underwater atomic tests CROSSROADS-BAKER (1946) and HARDTACK I YAHOO (1958) did not generate tsunamis.[38]

However, according to physicist Rex Richardson: "A well-placed nuclear weapon of yield in the range of 20 MT to 50 MT near a seacoast could certainly couple enough energy to equal the 2011 tsunami, and perhaps much more. Taking advantage of the rising sea-floor amplification effect, tsunami waves reaching 100 meters [330 feet] in height are possible."[39]

The facts indicate nuclear tsunamis are possible and could be a real threat.

The atomic tests cited by Spriggs to disprove nuclear tsunamis, CROSSROADS-BAKER and HARDTACK I YAHOO, utilized atomic bombs of yield 10-20 kilotons—5,000-10,000 times less powerful than POSEIDON's TSAR-like bomb of yield 100 megatons (100,000 kilotons). And these relatively low-yield atomic tests, while they did not create tsunamis, did double the height of ocean waves, flooding local atolls.[40]

Conventional high-explosives have raised, perhaps not tsunamis, but highly destructive waves. For example, on December 6, 1917, the French munitions ship SS Mont-Blanc exploded in Halifax, Nova Scotia, killing and injuring over 10,000 and leveling buildings out to a half-mile

---

Commitments: 1958-1983 (Washington, DC: October 1984) may be read at https://centerforsecuritypolicy.org/wp-content/uploads/2017/08/GAC-Report-Executive-Summary.pdf

[37] Dave Mosher, "A Physicist Says Blowing Up Nuclear Weapons In The Ocean To Trigger Tsunamis Would Be Completely Stupid" Business Insider (May 14, 2017).

[38] Ibid.

[39] Tom Davidson, "Vladimir Putin Unveils Underwater Poseidon Drone That Carries Nuclear Warhead Capable Of Causing 300ft Tsunamis" Online Reporter (May 18, 2018).

[40] Dave Mosher, "Putin's Nuclear 'Doomsday Machine' Could Trigger 300-foot Nuclear Tsunamis…" Business Insider (April 24, 2018). U.S. Navy, *Operation Crossroads: Bikini Atoll* (U.S. Navy Historical Center, October 24, 2012).

radius. Moreover: "A tsunami created by the blast wiped out the community of the Mi'kmag First Nation who had lived in the tufts cove area for generations."[41]

The Halifax explosion was estimated equivalent to 2.9 kilotons.[42] This is about 15,000-30,000 times less powerful than a 100-megaton POSEIDON warhead.

World War II research in Project Seal found that it is possible to "create a destructive wave" using conventional high-explosives equivalent to 2.2 kilotons.[43]

Nonetheless, while nuclear tsunamis are possible, there are good reasons to doubt that tsunamis are the real purpose of POSEIDON.

Is POSEIDON A Ruse?

Strangely for what was once represented as a secret super-weapon, Moscow has gone to extraordinary lengths to make sure the West knows about POSEIDON. Dictator Putin has described POSEIDON to a world television audience.[44] Photos, graphics, and diagrams of the POSEIDON prototype undergoing testing have been published by Russian news agency TASS.[45]

Russia has released vital statistics about POSEIDON. The robot-sub is nuclear powered. POSEIDON is advertised as having a speed of 100 knots and a depth of over 1 kilometer, supposedly making the robot-sub unstoppable.[46]

A 100-megaton POSEIDON could conceivably produce a tsunami, as described by the Russians, if detonated off the U.S. coast. A robot submarine could certainly transport a 100-megaton bomb like TSAR, weighing 30 tons.

But POSEIDON is not really practical as a weapon system or as a doomsday machine.

U.S. satellites would see POSEIDON leaving port for sinking by missiles, aircraft, and torpedoes. Even if the doomsday robot-bomb is intended to exact revenge after a nuclear exchange has destroyed U.S. satellites and the U.S. Navy, it likely would be a high priority target destroyed during the first salvos of a nuclear war.

Even if POSEIDON could survive a nuclear exchange and penetrate the screen of U.S. aircraft and attack submarines hunting for this top priority target, it would be a non-optimal way of attacking the United States.

---

[41] "Halifax Explosion" Wikipedia and Lois Kernaghan and Richard Foot in *The Canadian Encyclopedia* (1985).

[42] Ibid.

[43] Thomas Leech, *Project Seal: The Generation of Waves by Means of Explosives* (New Zealand: Department of Scientific and Industrial Research, December 18, 1950).

[44] Vladimir Isachenkov, "Putin Boasts of New Russian Nuclear Weapons: 'You Listen To Us Now'" Washington Times (March 1, 2018).

[45] www.youtube.com/watch?v=dOB_IdTeen4

[46] Ibid.

A 100-megaton weapon would do tremendous damage by blast, thermal effects, and tsunamis. But the damage radius of all these effects would not be enough to destroy more than a fraction of the entire east coast.

The alleged chief mission of the underwater doomsday bomb is to flood and contaminate the populous U.S. seaboard with radioactive fallout. But the prevailing winds and weather on the U.S. east coast moves from west to east—out to sea.[47]

Radioactive fallout is the effect that could cover the most territory. Fallout needs weather to be on its side if it is to be an effective lethal mechanism. Weather works against maximizing fallout effects on the U.S. east coast.[48]

Weather moves in the right direction for maximizing fallout effects from the U.S. west coast.[49]

However, the Los Angeles-San Diego corridor is not nearly as high priority to Russian targeteers as the Washington, DC-New York City corridor. Washington-New York is the locus of government and military leadership and control, and the heartland of elite society and civilization. While Washington is the capitol of the United States, New York is the capitol of the West.

Vladivostok is the only big Russian naval base in the Pacific to support POSEIDON and would be heavily targeted by the U.S. in a nuclear exchange, because of the presence of the Russian Pacific Fleet and large numbers of ballistic missile submarines. Traveling from Vladivostok across the vast Pacific to the U.S. west coast would be much harder for the robot-sub than crossing the Atlantic.

Russian ballistic missile submarines can strike the United States launching from their berths in Vladivostok. The warheads from a single Russian ballistic missile submarine, targeted for ground-contact bursts on U.S. cities, would inflict blast, thermal, and fallout effects collectively more lethal and damaging than a single 100-megaton warhead detonated off the coast. In every respect, in reliability and effectiveness, a single Russian ballistic missile submarine is already a far better doomsday weapon than Russia's robot-sub.

Attacking across either ocean is almost certain to be a suicide mission for POSEIDON, that would probably be sunk before it gets far from port. The robot-sub and its 100-megaton bomb, destroyed in or near port, could pose a greater doomsday threat to Russia than to the United States.

Bottom-line is that Russia's scheme for a doomsday robotic submarine makes no military sense, not even as a vengeance weapon. Nuclear tsunamis may be an elaborate ruse to conceal the real purpose of POSEIDON and its 100-megaton TSAR warhead.

---

[47] See projected nuclear fallout patterns over U.S. in Ken Jorgustin, "US Nuclear Target Map" Modern Survival Blog (March 18, 2015) https://modernsurvivalblog.com/nuclear/us-nuclear-target-map/
[48] Ibid.
[49] Ibid.

Anti-Submarine Warfare (ASW)

"Maskirovka" is an official and diligently practiced dimension of Russian military doctrine that seeks to achieve strategic and technological surprise by concealment and disinformation.[50]

Dictator Putin and Russian military commentary on POSEIDON lists its missions as:
--Making nuclear tsunamis to flood and radioactively contaminate U.S. coasts;
--Destroying U.S. naval bases and fortified submarine pens;
--Destroying U.S. aircraft carriers.

As explained above, POSEIDON is not really militarily necessary or practical for any of these missions. Russian nuclear missiles and bombers can already blast and radioactively contaminate U.S. cities coastal or otherwise, destroy U.S. naval bases and fortified submarine pens, and attack deployed U.S. aircraft carriers.

The only mission not mentioned for POSEIDON, the most obvious one, is attacking U.S. ballistic missile submarines (SSBNs) on patrol, hiding at sea.

During the Cold War, the USSR eventually achieved the ability to destroy all or most U.S. ICBMs, strategic bombers, and SSBNs in port by a surprise nuclear attack on their bases—but not submarines at sea. Many analysts credit the survivability of U.S. SSBNs at sea with deterring the USSR from launching World War III.[51]

The U.S. SSBN fleet during the 1980s Cold War numbered 36-41 vessels.[52]

Today, U.S. ICBMs, strategic bombers, and submarines in port are much more vulnerable to a Russian surprise nuclear attack than during the Cold War.[53] Today's Trident SSBN fleet numbers only 14 vessels, scheduled to decline to 12 Columbia SSBNs in the future.[54] On any given day, half of U.S. ballistic missile submarines are in port, and half patrolling at sea.

On a day-to-day basis, the most credibly survivable leg of the entire U.S. nuclear Triad amounts to just 7 ballistic missile submarines, in the future declining to 6 SSBNs.
What if POSEIDON, a nuclear-powered drone, is intended to be always on patrol at sea, rarely or never returning to port—always tailing U.S. SSBNs to destroy them, on command, in a surprise attack? Advances in sensors and artificial intelligence make such a mission for POSEIDON plausible.

---

[50] "Maskirovka" *Soviet Military Encyclopedia* (Moscow: Voyenizdat, 1978 in Russian). Willard Frank and Philip Gillette, *Soviet Military Doctrine From Lenin To Gorbachev* (Westport: Greenwood Publishing Group, 1992). Levi Maxey, "Threat Report 2018: Russia's Military Doctrine of Deception and Denial" thecipherbrief.com (June 2018). "Russian Military Deception" Wikipedia.

[51] Dr. Peter Vincent Pry, *The Strategic Nuclear Balance: And Why It Matters* (New York and London: Crane Russak, Taylor & Francis, 1990).

[52] Ibid. "Ballistic Missile Submarine" Wikipedia.

[53] Dr. Peter Vincent Pry, "Mutual Assured Destruction (MAD) No Longer Mutual: U.S. Unilaterally Vulnerable" Family Security Matters (March 14, 2018).

[54] Congressional Research Service, *Navy Columbia (SSBN-826) Class Ballistic Missile Submarine Program* (January 12, 2018).

The POSEIDON prototype operates out of a mother ship, which will be fatal for the robot-sub if it is intended to deploy from port in wartime, as explained earlier. However, POSEIDON could deploy in peacetime for protracted patrols or lingering outside U.S. ports, like a mobile underwater mine, hunting U.S. SSBNs until D-Day.

POSEIDON makes more sense as a "release and forget" independent killer, since the mother ship would be destroyed if anywhere in the neighborhood of POSEIDON's blast.

U.S. submarines are still stealthier and more elusive than Russian subs. But a 100-megaton warhead detonated underwater—because a nuclear shockwave couples to water far more efficiently than to air, and travels through water faster and farther—would have an enormous lethal radius against submarines.

Unclassified data from the YAHOO and BAKER underwater nuclear tests proves the vulnerability of submarines and even heavily armored ships to a nuclear shockwave transmitted through water. According to the Department of Defense in *The Effects of Nuclear Weapons*:

"An underwater shock acting on the hull of a ship tends to cause distortion of the hull below the waterline and rupture the shell plating, thus producing leaks as well as severely stressing the ship's framing. The underwater shock also leads to a rapid movement in both horizontal and vertical directions. This motion causes damage by shock to components and equipment…Main feed lines, main steam lines, shafting and boiler brickwork within the ship are especially sensitive to shock. Due to the effects of inertia, the supporting members of foundations of heavy components, such as engines and boilers, are likely to collapse or become distorted. Lighter or inadequately fastened articles will be thrown about with great violence, causing damage to themselves, to bulkheads, and to other equipment."

"For most cases of underwater explosion the water shock will be the important factor in determining damage," according to *The Effects of Nuclear Weapons*.[55]

---

[55]Samuel Glasstone and Philip J. Dolan editors, *The Effects of Nuclear Weapons* (Washington, DC: Department of Defense, 1977).

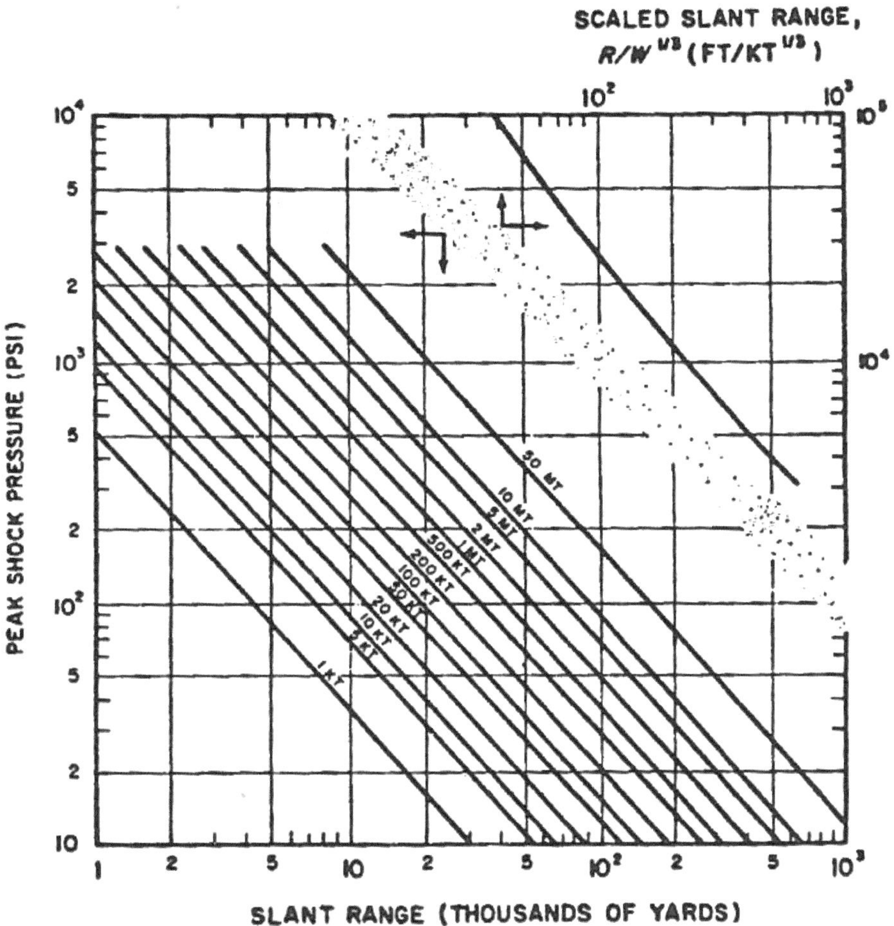

Figure 5.1. Shock wave peak pressure from deep underwater burst. *Source*: Samuel Glasstone and Philip J. Dolan (eds.), *The Effects of Nuclear Weapons* (Washington, DC: Department of Defense and Energy Research and Development Administration, 1977), p. 271.

Table 5.2
Warhead Lethal Radius against Submarines

Yield Kilotons	Lethal Radius 1,000 PSI		Lethal Radius 300 PSI	
	Nautical Miles	Kilometers	Nautical Miles	Kilometers
50	1.0	1.8	3.0	5.5
100	1.4	2.2	3.6	6.6
200	1.6	3.0	4.6	8.6
500	2.2	4.1	5.9	11.0
750	2.5	4.6	7.4	13.7
1,000	2.9	5.4	8.9	16.5
5,000	4.9	9.1	13.8	25.6
10,000	6.4	11.9	17.3	32.0
25,000	10.2	18.9	24.2	45.0

Source: Estimated from shock wave peak pressure curves in Samuel Glasstone and Philip J. Dolan (eds.), *The Effects of Nuclear Weapons* (Washington, DC: Department of Defense and Energy Research and Development Administration, 1977), p. 271.

Even assuming U.S. SSBNs are very robust, hardened to survive an underwater shockwave of 300 PSI (three times harder than the Atlas-F ICBM missile silo), the lethal radius of a 100 megaton warhead could be 100 kilometers or more. An atmospheric shockwave would destroy brick buildings at 5 PSI. An underwater shockwave from 100 megatons could deliver 5 PSI to a radius of several hundred kilometers.[56]

Russian SSBNs need not be at risk from POSEIDON because their intercontinental-range missiles enable them to strike the U.S. from port or from their heavily defended bastion areas near port, in the Barents Sea and Sea of Okhotsk. U.S. SSBNs armed with intermediate-range missiles must be in mid-ocean to reach their targets in Russia.[57]

While POSEIDON's real mission might be anti-submarine warfare, there is an even better additional or alternative mission for revival of a 100-megaton warhead like TSAR—including a better way to perform the ASW and doomsday missions. Indeed, POSEIDON might be an elaborate ruse, a disinformation campaign concealing the real mission for their 100-megaton warhead—in order to achieve decisive technological surprise.

Electromagnetic Pulse (EMP) Attack

The most militarily sensible mission for a 100-megaton warhead like TSAR is a high-altitude electromagnetic pulse (EMP) attack.

A 100-megaton weapon detonated at high-altitude, in outer space, would be the perfect anti-satellite weapon. X-rays, gamma rays, neutrons, and pumping the Van Allen belts with ionized particles would sweep the heavens of satellites vital to U.S. military and commercial operations. EMP would damage and destroy satellite ground stations. U.S. domination of the "high frontier" that is the key to U.S. high-tech military supremacy would vanish at a single blow.[58]

A 100-megaton weapon detonated 400 kilometers above the center of the U.S. would generate a manmade geomagnetic-superstorm, like lightning striking everywhere nationwide simultaneously, but far more powerful than lightning. Such a man-created electronic storm would deluge North America with the kind of powerful long-wave E3 EMPs that directly destroy even the biggest transformers and generators. It would plunge the entire nation into protracted, perhaps permanent, blackout.[59]

Russia already has what it calls Super-EMP weapons, designed to generate powerful short-wave E1 EMP that would destroy most electronics, and put big transformers and generators at risk

---

[56]Dr. Peter Vincent Pry, *Nuclear Wars: Exchanges and Outcomes*, Chapter 5 "Submarine Survival" (New York and London: Crane Russak, Taylor & Francis, 1990). Glasstone and Dolan, op. cit. Atlas-F ICBM silo 100 PSI see "SM-65 Atlas" Wikipedia (August 2015).

[57] Trident II D-5 the longest range sub-launched ballistic missile deployed by the U.S. can fly 7,360 kilometers. "Trident II D-5 Fleet Ballistic Missile" Federation of American Scientists https://fas.org/nuke/guide/usa/slbm/d-5.htm

[58] For EMP effects on the electric power grid, civilian critical infrastructures, military C3I and forces, and satellites as described in this section see www.firstempcommission.org: Congressional EMP Commission, *Assessing The Threat From EMP Attack—Executive Report* (2017); Congressional EMP Commission, *Report of the Commission to Assess the Threat to the United States from Electromagnetic Pulse (EMP) Attack: Critical National Infrastructures* (2008); Congressional EMP Commission, *Report of the Commission to Assess the Threat to the United States from Electromagnetic Pulse (EMP) Attack: Executive Summary* (2004). See also Pry, *Nuclear Wars* op. cit., "EMP Attacks" pp. 24-27.

[59] Ibid.

indirectly.[60]   But these low-yield (1-10 kilotons) Super-EMP weapons would not make long-wave E3 EMPs as powerful as the TSAR.

The TSAR combined with Super-EMP weapons would cover the electromagnetic spectrum with redundant electronic mass destruction—EMP overkill perhaps, but historically and doctrinally mass and firepower overkill is Russia's way of war.

An EMP attack on North America could supplement or substitute for POSEIDON's anti-submarine warfare mission. EMP could be the best ASW weapon.

U.S. ballistic missile submarines at sea cannot launch without receiving an Emergency Action Message (EAM) from the president authorizing missile launches. The EAM also includes an unlocking code to arm nuclear warheads. Thus, SSBNs cannot execute a nuclear strike without receiving the EAM.[61]

An EMP attack could destroy or degrade the satellites, land-based VLF communications systems, TACAMO aircraft, and other redundant means of strategic command and control used to convey EAMs to submarines hiding at sea. Severing their communications links to the National Command Authority would neutralize U.S. submarines, rendering them useless.[62]

EMP could also be used to attack submarines on patrol at sea directly.

A 100-megaton warhead detonated at 400 kilometers altitude over the ocean would cover an area 2,200 kilometers in radius, a zone nearly as large as North America, with powerful E3 EMP that would penetrate the ocean depths and possibly couple into submarines on patrol, damaging or destroying their electronics. Submarines would be especially vulnerable when deploying their very long antennae—which they need to do precisely when trying to receive Emergency Action Messages.[63]

---

[60] Ibid. *Russia: Nuclear Response To America Is Possible Using Super-EMP Factor* CEP20061108358006, Aleksey Vaschenko, "A Nuclear Response To America Is Possible" Zavtra (November 1, 2006). Dr. Peter Vincent Pry, *The Long Sunday* "Super-EMP Weapons" (Washington, DC; Center for Security Policy for EMP Task Force on National and Homeland Security, 2016).

[61] *The Long Sunday* op. cit. p. 59. *Nuclear Wars* op. cit. pp. 24-27. Sebastien Roblin, "The Deadliest Aircraft in the U.S. Military Arsenal You Have Never Heard Of" The National Interest (April 23, 2017). "Nuclear Launch Codes" https://www.everything2.com/title/Nuclear+launch+codes

[62] Ibid.

[63] Ibid. *The Long Sunday* op. cit. pp. 15, 59.

ELECTROMAGNETIC PULSE (EMP) FIELD RADIUS ON EARTH'S SURFACE FROM NUCLEAR WEAPON DETONATED AT GIVEN HEIGHT OF BURST(HOB)

(Kilometers)

HOB	EMP Radius	HOB	EMP Radius	HOB	EMP Radius
30	602*	160	1,391	290	1,873
40	696	170	1,434	300	1,905
50	778	180	1,476	310	1,937
60	852	190	1,516	320	1,968
70	920	200	1,556	330	1,998
80	984	210	1,594	340	2,028
90	1,044	220	1,632	350	2,058
100	1,100	230	1,668	360	2,087
110	1,153	240	1,704	370	2,116
120	1,205	250	1,739	380	2,144
130	1,254	260	1,774	390	2,172
140	1,301	270	1,807	400	2,200**
150	1,347	280	1,841		

Calculated from Radius $= 110 (\sqrt{HOB})$ in kilometers

*   Radius exceeds distance from New York to Washington

**   Radius covers all of continental United States

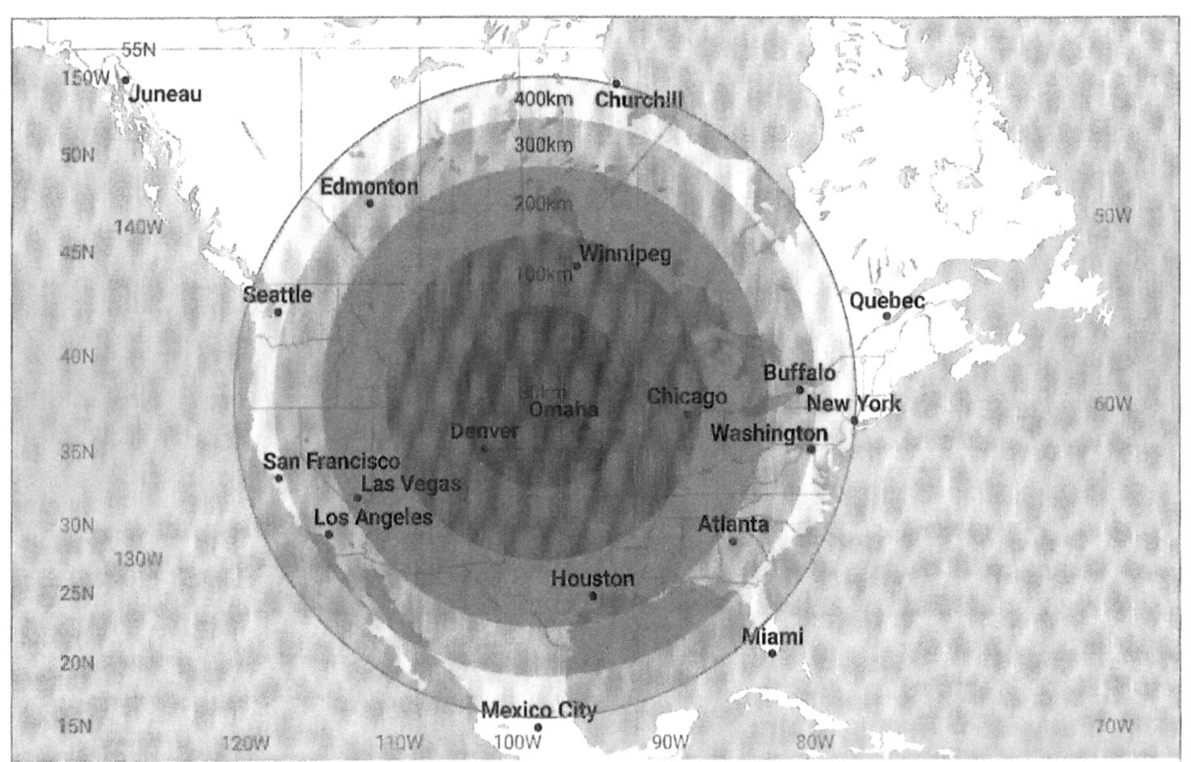

NUCLEAR HEMP AREA COVERAGE
NUCLEAR EMP ATTACK SCENARIOS

EMP field coverage increases with increasing height-of-burst. A balloon or jet aircraft could loft a nuclear warhead to an altitude of 30 kilometers which, targeted over New York City, would also cover Washington, D.C., New York State, New Jersey, Pennsylvania, Virginia, Maryland, Delaware, and most of New England

Only a few 100-megaton warheads, with their enormous E3 EMP fields, would be needed to cover the most likely oceanic patrol areas for U.S. submarines.

The TSAR could be disguised as a satellite and delivered by a Space-Launch Vehicle (SLV) over the South Pole to evade U.S. National Missile Defenses--making a surprise EMP attack. This is exactly what Moscow planned to do during the Cold War with a secret weapon called the Fractional Orbital Bombardment System (FOBS).[64]

North Korea appears to have revived the FOBS, orbiting two satellites over the U.S. from south polar trajectories.[65] Moscow is reclaiming its original idea. Russian dictator Putin recently boasted that one of his new nuclear super-weapons—the Satan II heavy ICBM—is capable of making a surprise attack against the U.S. over the South Pole.[66]

Satan-II could probably deliver the TSAR to make a surprise south polar EMP attack to permanently blackout North America. Russia's Proton-M SLV is highly reliable and is also capable of delivering the massive 30-ton TSAR warhead on a fractional orbit to North America. A modernized version of the TSAR could probably be designed weighing significantly less than the original TSAR's 30 tons.

A surprise EMP attack could enable Russia to win a nuclear war with a single blow by paralyzing U.S. military forces and C3I—perhaps this is the real reason for the return of the TSAR.

A high-altitude EMP attack by the TSAR would also, more assuredly than an underwater detonation, be doomsday for the United States by causing a protracted blackout of U.S. life-sustaining critical infrastructures. The Congressional EMP Commission warns that a nationwide blackout lasting one year could kill 90 percent of the population through societal collapse and starvation.[67]

POSEIDON and its experimental prototype could be part of a disinformation campaign to conceal the real military purpose of the TSAR, while Russia still reaps the diplomatic and psychological benefits from putting the West on notice that Moscow has a 100-megaton doomsday bomb.

Russia's Doomsday Way Of Diplomacy And War

Is Russia's POSEIDON robot-sub project and its TSAR-like 100-megaton warhead all disinformation? Unfortunately, almost certainly not.

---

[64] Miroslav Gyurosi, *The Soviet Fractional Orbital Bombardment System Program* (Air Power Australia Technical Report APA-TR-2010-0101, updated April 2012).

[65] Hearing "Empty Threat or Serious Danger: Assessing North Korea's Risk To The Homeland" before the U.S. House of Representatives, Committee on Homeland Security, Subcommittee on Oversight and Management Efficiency, Statement for the Record by Dr. William Graham and Dr. Peter Vincent Pry, "North Korea Nuclear EMP Attack: An Existential Threat" Congressional EMP Commission (October 12, 2017).

[66] "Russia Tests New Ballistic Missile That Putin Says Can Strike Anywhere On Earth" Associated Press (March 30, 2018).

[67] Staff Paper, *Congressional EMP Commission Examples From Testimony And Reports That Fatalities Could Be High Numbering Millions 90 Percent Of National Population* (EMP Task Force On National And Homeland Security).

Moscow has an affinity for doomsday weapons—and for revealing their existence in a crisis.

TSAR was tested in part as an act of nuclear diplomacy, one year after Soviet Premier Nikita Khrushchev pounded his shoe on his desk (October 12, 1960) to seize the floor at the United Nations and warn the West not to provoke the USSR. "We will bury you!" Khrushchev had repeatedly warned during this period, when both sides were building nuclear fallout shelters and nuclear war was considered imminent.[68]

The dramatic TSAR test and the Cuban Missile Crisis were contributing factors to the first arms control agreement, the Limited Test Ban Treaty, signed by the U.S. and USSR on October 10, 1963, that prohibited nuclear testing in the atmosphere. This began an arms control process that enabled the USSR to catch-up and eventually surpass the United States in nuclear offensive and defensive capabilities.[69]

30 years after TSAR, and after the dissolution of the USSR in 1991, Russia continued practicing doomsday diplomacy with another doomsday machine—DEAD HAND.

After the fall of the Soviet Union, when Russia was at its weakest, during the September-October 1993 coup attempt by hardliners against Russian President Boris Yeltsin, Moscow conducted a major military and strategic forces "exercise" called TSENTER. TSENTER in fact probably was not an exercise, but a real mobilization of conventional and nuclear forces. The Russian General Staff, still deeply paranoid and fearful of the West, mobilized to deter aggression or intervention by the United States—preparing even to launch a preemptive nuclear strike, if necessary, against America. Washington, thinking the Cold War over, was oblivious to the danger.[70]

Amidst the crisis, on October 8, 1993, the New York Times broke a story that Russia has a doomsday computer called "DEAD HAND" (officially PERIMETR) that would automatically launch strategic nuclear forces, in the event that Russia's president and top military leaders are killed in a surprise attack. Russian General Varfolomey Korobushin, former Deputy Chief of Staff of the Strategic Rocket Forces, was among the high-ranking sources warning the West about DEAD HAND.[71]

Most analysts assess that the evidence really does support the existence of Russia's DEAD HAND system for launching a nuclear doomsday automatically. In 2011, Russia's Chief of the Strategic Rocket Forces, General Sergey Karakaev, affirmed the continued existence of DEAD HAND, which reportedly is being upgraded in 2018.[72]

---

[68] For an example of U.S. reaction to the TSAR test see: "Blast Assailed On Capitol Hill As Soviet Act Of Intimidation" Associated Press for St. Louis Post-Dispatch (October 30, 1961).

[69] Keith Payne, *The Fallacies of Cold War Deterrence and a New Direction* (National Institute for Public Policy, 2001). Keith Payne, *The Great American Gamble: Deterrence Theory and Practice from the Cold War to the Twenty-First Century* (National Institute for Public Policy, 2008).

[70] Dr. Peter Vincent Pry, *War Scare: Russia And America On The Nuclear Brink*, Part IV "The October Coup" (Praeger, 1999).

[71] Ibid. "Russia Has 'Doomsday' Machine U.S. Expert Says" New York Times (October 8, 1993).

[72] Henry Holloway, "Russia Upgrading Its Dreaded Doomsday Device 'Dead Hand' Which Fires All Its Nukes At Once" Daily Star (March 28, 2018).

DEAD HAND is described as a system for automatically launching a retaliatory strike, based on sensors that would detect blast and thermal effects from nuclear explosions on Russian territory.[73]

Another Russian doomsday machine is known to exist called VRYAN (the Russian acronym for "Surprise Nuclear Missile Attack"). VRYAN, a computer, would predict, based on thousands of intelligence indicators, when the U.S. is preparing to make a nuclear attack—so Moscow can launch a preemptive strike.[74]

Let us hope DEAD HAND and VRYAN are not wired together to make a preemptive first strike—automatically.

So why resurrect the TSAR now? What crisis is at hand that has moved Moscow to reveal the existence of its latest doomsday weapon, POSEIDON, and its 100-megaton bomb?

That the answer is not obvious signifies just how dangerously unpredictable is Vladimir Putin's Russia. While few in the West see any crisis that would warrant nuclear war, Moscow obviously thinks otherwise.

A warning to those who would try to impose a Syrian no-fly zone on Russia, who would have the U.S. intervene in Ukraine against Russia, who would wage economic warfare to try dethroning Vladimir Putin—be mindful that Russia's way of warfare is total annihilation.

Historically, since Tsar Ivan the Terrible (1565-1572) Moscow's way of warfare has been doomsday for the Mongols, for Napoleon, for Hitler, and for "enemies" domestic too.

Ivan the Terrible exiled, tortured, and executed 12,000 of his own nobles at the hands of his roving terror henchmen, the Oprichniki. Imperial Russia's secret police, the Okhrana, through their ruthless cruelty gave birth to Vladimir Lenin and helped set the stage for the Russian Revolution. Lenin's Red Terror and Stalin's Great Terror, through the Cheka and NKVD (predecessors to Putin's KGB) killed 20 million innocents.[75]

Moscow has been a doomsday machine to its own people. The Kremlin is no less dangerous to us.

How dangerously paranoid is a regime that thinks it must imprison an all-girl punk rock band for praying to the Virgin Mary to save Russia from Vladimir Putin?[76]

Pussy Riot was right to pray—and so should we that President Trump can find a way to de-escalate and reset relations with Russia on a more constructive course, or at least on a course heading away from doomsday.

Cocky fools, unread in Russian history, who are eager to "challenge Russia" and "poke the Bear" over matters merely tangential to core U.S. interests are no friends of the Free World or of collective humanity at this dangerous hour.

---

[73] Ibid. *War Scare*, op. cit., p. 153. Bruce Blair, *The Logic of Accidental Nuclear War* (Brookings, 1993).

[74] *War Scare*, op. cit., "Operation Vryan" pp. 9-15.

[75] Robert Conquest, *The Great Terror* (2007).

[76] "Russian Female Punk Band Pussy Riot Gets 2 Years…" CBS/AP (August 17, 2012).

The challenge President Trump inherited from President Obama is extraordinarily difficult. Appeasement will only encourage Russian aggression. Trump must be strong during one of the most perilous times in U.S. history, when Obama has left U.S. military forces and the nuclear deterrent at their weakest in decades, while avoiding confrontation at least until the U.S. can rebuild its strength.

Ironically, President Obama's neglecting U.S. nuclear deterrence while questing for a utopian "world without nuclear weapons" has bequeathed to President Trump and our children a dystopian legacy--the New Cold War and Russia's doomsday bomb.

What Is To Be Done?

President Trump should sign the draft executive order submitted to President Obama by the Congressional EMP Commission, but ignored for 8 years, to protect the nation from nuclear EMP attack. The EMP Commission's long-neglected specific recommendations to protect the electric power grid and other life-sustaining critical infrastructures should be implemented on a crash emergency basis.

EMP protection of the electric grid and other national critical infrastructures could be quickly accomplished as part of President Trump's plan for critical infrastructure modernization. The EMP Commission estimated in 2008 that the national electric grid could be EMP hardened in a few years for about $2 billion. Much could be accomplished in 6 months.

Revive President Ronald Reagan's Strategic Defense Initiative and deploy on a crash emergency basis Brilliant Pebbles space-based defenses that can intercept hundreds of missiles during boost-phase, midcourse, and re-entry phase. SDI and Brilliant Pebbles were both canceled by the Clinton Administration for ideological reasons to preserve the principle of Mutual Assured Destruction (MAD).

Ambassador Henry Cooper, former Director of the Strategic Defense Initiative, estimates that Brilliant Pebbles could be deployed, if given high priority, before the end of President Trump's second term at a cost of $10-20 billion.

SDI's Brilliant Pebbles— combined with EMP protection of U.S. critical infrastructures— could render nuclear missiles obsolete, work a revolution in military technology shifting the advantage from offense to defense, thereby stabilizing the strategic balance and replacing MAD with a new principle, call it Strategic Assured National Existence (SANE).

Killing nuclear missiles instead of enemy populations, defending the American people from nuclear EMP and other effects instead of avenging our dead, is more consistent with the Judeo-Christian values of Western Civilization. Strategically and politically SANE is a more credible and practical solution than MAD to the challenge of doomsday machines like POSEIDON.

Nonetheless, as long as nuclear missiles and bombers exist, the U.S. must continue to modernize its strategic offensive nuclear forces to deter and defeat all possible adversaries. U.S. modernization should not be chiefly of new delivery systems, as is currently planned, but of a new advanced generation of nuclear weapons—including U.S. versions of Super-EMP nuclear weapons. The $700 billion dollar price tag for modernizing MAD should not leave the U.S. technologically inferior to Russia in any category of nuclear offensive capabilities.

The existential threat posed by nuclear weapons to civilization demands redundant and mutually-reinforcing levels of preparedness, including preparedness to:

--Deter nuclear attack with the threat of retaliation;
--Preempt nuclear attack by a disarming strike;
--Defeat nuclear attack by active defenses (SDI's Brilliant Pebbles);
--Defeat nuclear attack by passive defenses (EMP hardening, civil defense);

POSEIDON should be preemptively destroyed if deployed on operational patrols off U.S. coasts or to trail U.S. submarines and aircraft carriers. Moscow should be warned that Washington will not tolerate an autonomous artificially intelligent doomsday machine roaming U.S. coastal waters or the world's oceans.

Strangely, those who would "poke the bear" by arming Ukraine and other provocative actions merely tangential to U.S. interests are silently complacent about existential threats to America—like EMP attack and POSEIDON.

Henry Kissinger warns in "How The Enlightenment Ends" (Atlantic, June 2018) that civilization may be threatened by the failure of governments to comprehend the potential dangers of Artificial Intelligence (AI), over-eager to exploit AI capabilities for defense:

"Philosophers and others in the field of the humanities who helped shape previous concepts of world order tend to be disadvantaged, lacking knowledge of AI's mechanisms or being overawed by its capacities. In contrast, the scientific world is impelled to explore the technical possibilities of its achievements, and the technological world is preoccupied with commercial vistas of fabulous scale. The incentive of both these worlds is to push the limits of discoveries rather than to comprehend them. And governance, insofar as it deals with the subject, is more likely to investigate AI's applications for security and intelligence than to explore the transformation of the human condition that it has begun to produce."

Almost before the ink from Kissinger's pen is dry, Moscow is testing its POSEIDON robot to deliver a 100-megaton bomb. *The combination of nuclear super-weapons and Artificial Intelligence is an unprecedented new threat that eclipses the invention of the atomic bomb—and that perhaps will end not only the Enlightenment, but Mankind.*

We need not resignedly accept, President Trump and the U.S. Navy can assertively veto, Russia's planned POSEIDON escalation of Mutual Assured Destruction. We can and should veto MAD itself with SANE.

Finally, saying "no" to Moscow—and if necessary sinking POSEIDON—could be the beginning of the end of the New Cold War. Russia respects strength. POSEIDON, like TSAR before it, could become an opportunity to seek a New Détente, and perhaps even achieve the rapprochement and real strategic partnership that should have replaced the old Cold War.

DR. PETER VINCENT PRY

Dr. Peter Vincent Pry is Executive Director of the EMP Task Force on National and Homeland Security, a Congressional Advisory Board dedicated to achieving protection of the United States from electromagnetic pulse (EMP), cyberattack, mass destruction terrorism and other threats to civilian critical infrastructures on an accelerted basis. Dr. Pry also is Director of the United States Nuclear Strategy Forum, an advisory board to Congress on policies to counter Weapons of Mass Destruction.

Dr. Pry served on the staffs of the Congressional Commission on the Strategic Posture of the United States (2008-2009); the Commission on the New Strategic Posture of the United States (2006-2008); and the Commission to Assess the Threat to the United States from Electromagnetic Pulse (EMP) Attack (2001-2017) as Chief of Staff.

Dr. Pry served as Professional Staff on the House Armed Services Committee (HASC) of the U.S. Congress, with portfolios in nuclear strategy, WMD, Russia, China, NATO, the Middle East, Intelligence, and Terrorism (1995-2001). While serving on the HASC, Dr. Pry was chief advisor to the Vice Chairman of the House Armed Services Committee and the Vice Chairman of the House Homeland Security Committee, and to the Chairman of the Terrorism Panel. Dr. Pry played a key role: running hearings in Congress that warned terrorists and rogue states could pose an EMP threat, establishing the Congressional EMP Commission, helping the Commission develop plans to protect the United States from EMP, and working closely with senior scientists who first discovered the nuclear EMP phenomenon.

Dr. Pry was an Intelligence Officer with the Central Intelligence Agency responsible for analyzing Soviet and Russian nuclear strategy, operational plans, military doctrine, threat perceptions, and developing U.S. paradigms for strategic warning (1985-1995). He also served as a Verification Analyst at the U.S. Arms Control and Disarmament Agency responsible for assessing Soviet compliance with strategic and military arms control treaties (1984-1985).

Dr. Pry has written numerous books on national security issues, including: *The Long Sunday…Nuclear EMP Attack Scenarios; Blackout Wars; Apocalypse Unknown: The Struggle To Protect America From An Electromagnetic Pulse Catastrophe; Electric Armageddon: Civil-Military Preparedness For An Electromagnetic Pulse Catastrophe; War Scare: Russia and America on the Nuclear Brink; Nuclear Wars: Exchanges and Outcomes; The Strategic Nuclear Balance: And Why It Matters*; and *Israel's Nuclear Arsenal*. Dr. Pry often appears on TV and radio as an expert on national security issues. The BBC made his book *War Scare* into a two-hour TV documentary *Soviet War Scare 1983* and his book *Electric Armageddon* was the basis for another TV documentary *Electronic Armageddon* made by the National Geographic.